Things That Go

By James Edward

Character illustrations by Jon Stuart

OXFORD
University Press

📖 READ

This book is about things that go!

There are lots of different things that go. Cars, buses and trains all help us to get from one place to another.

Trucks are used to transport goods. Tractors are used on farms.

Some cars are used in sport. They can go very fast!*

👥 ACTIVITY

- Point to the word *track* and ask children to sound-talk it (i.e. track becomes t-r-a-ck).

- Then ask children to blend the sounds together and say the word (i.e. t-r-a-ck becomes track).

- Ask children to write the word *track*. They could use magnetic letters, a whiteboard or a pencil and paper to write.

★ Tip

See the inside back cover for more guidance on sounds.

* The /a/ sound in the word *fast* will vary according to accent.

This car can go fast on a track.

📖 READ

Trains help us travel long distances. They travel along metal tracks or rails.

They can go very fast because there is no other traffic on the rails.

Nowadays most trains run on electric rails. But you can still sometimes see old steam engines puffing through the countryside.

👥 ACTIVITY

- Point to the word *shed* and ask children to sound-talk it (i.e. shed becomes sh-e-d).

- Then ask children to blend the sounds together and say the word (i.e. sh-e-d becomes shed).

- Read out the following sentence: *The train is chugging along the track.* Ask children to sound-talk the word *chugging* and then write the word.

It is puffing along to its shed.

📖 READ

Tractors are used on farms. They are used for jobs like ploughing fields, pulling trailers and spraying crops.

A tractor has two big wheels at the back and two smaller wheels at the front.

The big, back wheels help the tractor to travel over rough ground.

💬 TALK

- Tell children some farming facts:
  ○ The farmer ploughs the field before planting crops.
  ○ Wheat is grown on a farm and is milled into flour to make bread and pasta.
  ○ Potatoes are grown on a farm and can be used for making mashed potatoes and crisps.

👥 ACTIVITY

- Point to the word *along* and ask children to sound-talk it (i.e. along becomes a-l-o-ng).
- Then ask children to blend the sounds together and say the word (i.e. a-l-o-ng becomes along).

It can chug along in the mud.

READ

Diggers are machines that carry heavy loads from place to place.

They have big scooped buckets for digging up and carrying soil and rocks.

They have tracks as well as wheels. These are called caterpillar tracks. They can roll over bumpy ground.

ACTIVITY

- Point to the word *rocks* and ask children to sound-talk it (i.e. rocks becomes r-o-ck-s).
- Then ask children to blend the sounds together and say the word (i.e. r-o-ck-s becomes rocks).
- Can they think of any words that rhyme with *rocks* (e.g. socks, locks)?

thud

READ

Trucks are used to transport all sorts of goods. They often have to go very long distances.

Trucks can carry large and heavy things. They have lots of wheels to support the weight of the things they carry.

Very long trucks are called road trains.

This one has lots and lots of wheels!

TALK

- Ask children how many wheels they can see in the picture.
- Do they know any other names for trucks (e.g. lorry, tanker)?
- **Have some fun!** Ask children to imagine what it would be like to drive a big, long truck. Get them to describe their truck and talk about what they might be carrying in it.

📖 READ

There are lots of exciting things that go. Not all of them have engines or are powered by electricity.

Some are people-powered!

💬 TALK

- Ask children if they can think of any more things with wheels (e.g. a wheelchair, wheelbarrow).

👥 ACTIVITY

- Read the following sentence, and ask children to say the missing word: *Tiger is going … on his skateboard.* (clue: it rhymes with *last*). (fast)
- Ask children to write the word *fast*.

We can rush along.